ROB NOLASCO

SPEAKING
ELEMENTARY

OXFORD SUPPLEMENTARY SKILLS

SERIES EDITOR: ALAN MALEY

OXFORD UNIVERSITY PRESS

Oxford University Press
Walton Street, Oxford OX2 6DP

Oxford New York Toronto
Delhi Bombay Calcutta Madras Karachi
Petaling Jaya Singapore Hong Kong Tokyo
Nairobi Dar es Salaam Cape Town
Melbourne Auckland

and associated companies in
Berlin Ibadan

Oxford and *Oxford English* are trade marks of
Oxford University Press

ISBN 0 19 453408 1

© Oxford University Press 1987

First published 1987
Fourth impression 1991

Set by Promenade Graphics Ltd, Cheltenham.

Printed in Hong Kong

Illustrations by:

Judy Brown
Debi Gliori
David Murray

Studio and location photography:

Rob Judges

The publishers would like to thank the following for
permission to reproduce photographs:

The Ancient Art and Architecture Collection
(Ronald Sheridan's Photo-Library)
Austin Rover Group Ltd
Barnaby's Picture Library
BBC Hulton Picture Library
The Bridgeman Art Library
Camera Press Ltd
J Allan Cash Photolibrary
Colorific!
Sally and Richard Greenhill
The Hutchison Library
Japan Information Centre, London
Land Rover Ltd
ORPIX Operation Raleigh
Rex Features Ltd
Syndication International
The Tate Gallery, London
Topham Picture Library
Westward Ho Adventure Holidays Ltd

ACKNOWLEDGEMENTS

I should like to thank the following people:

Lois for her encouragement, support and help; Keith Ricketts and Lois Arthur for allowing themselves to be recorded.

Acknowledgements are also made to:

Edward de Bono and William Collins and Sons Ltd for extracts from *Tactics, The Art and Science of Success*; Guinness Superlatives Ltd for extracts from *The Guinness Book of Records* (1985); Studs Terkel and Hodder and Stoughton Ltd for an extract from *American Dreams Lost and Found*; James Thurber and Hamish Hamilton Ltd for 'The Little Girl and the Wolf' from *Vintage Thurber Volume 1*.

Task 2 in 'Dreams to remember' (Unit 7.1) is based on an idea from *Drama Techniques in Language Learning* by Alan Maley and Alan Duff. 'Competitiveness' (Unit 8.3) was inspired by the work of Kathy Bailey.

CONTENTS

FOREWORD

This series covers the four skill areas of Listening, Speaking, Reading and Writing at four levels — elementary, intermediate, upper-intermediate and advanced. Although we have decided to retain the traditional division of language use into the 'four skills', the skills are not treated in total isolation. In any given book the skill being dealt with serves as the *focus* of attention and is always interwoven with and supported by other skills. This enables teachers to concentrate on skills development without losing touch with the more complex reality of language use.

Our authors have had in common the following principles, that material should be:

- creative — both through author-creativity leading to interesting materials, and through their capacity to provoke creative responses from students;
- interesting — both for their cognitive and affective content, and for the activities required of the learners;
- fluency-focused — bringing in accuracy work only in so far as it is necessary to the completion of an activity;
- task-based — rather than engaging in closed exercise activities, to use tasks with pay-offs for the learners;
- problem-solving focused — so as to engage students in cognitive effort and thus provoke meaningful interaction;
- humanistic — in the sense that the materials speak to and interrelate with the learners as real people and engage them in interaction grounded in their own experience;
- learning-centred — by ensuring that the materials promote learning and help students to develop their own strategies for learning. This is in opposition to the view that a pre-determined content is taught and identically internalized by all students. In our materials we do not expect input to equal intake.

By ensuring continuing consultation between and among authors at different levels, and by piloting the materials, the levels have been established on a pragmatic basis. The fact that the authors, between them, share a wide and varied body of experience has made this possible without losing sight of the need to pitch materials and tasks at an attainable level while still allowing for the spice of challenge.

There are three main ways in which these materials can be used:

- as a supplement to a core course book;
- as self-learning material. Most of the books can be used on an individual basis with a minimum of teacher guidance, though the interactive element is thereby lost.
- as modular course material. A teacher might, for instance, combine intermediate *Listening* and *Speaking* books with upper-intermediate *Reading* and elementary *Writing* with a class which had a good passive knowledge of English but which needed a basic grounding in writing skills. (*Alan Maley, Madras 1986*)

INTRODUCTION TO THE TEACHER

Aims of the material

The aim of the material is to provide fluency-based practice material in the areas of oral performance most relevant to adult general-purpose learners of English at elementary level. These are:

- maintaining and developing simple conversations on everyday topics
- exchanging personal views and opinions
- sharing experiences
- collecting and passing on information orally
- telling a short story or anecdote
- giving a short talk
- collaborating in getting something done in English.

The emphasis on fluency means the tasks involve the learner in using whatever linguistic and non-linguistic resources he/she has to the limit. Emphasis is on tasks which give learners:

- the experience of using English in a realistic way (authenticity of response)
- the chance to express *their own* ideas, attitudes and emotions (so that they are motivated to *use* English)
- the opportunity of using language for a purpose (so that mistakes matter).

In other words learners need the opportunity to learn to communicate in English by doing just that in the 'sheltered environment' of the classroom. Fluency practice of this sort is not available in many coursebooks and this material should be regarded as a necessary supplement for teachers who want to develop their learners' ability to use English in verbal communication outside the classroom.

The materials

There are eight units of practice material and an outline of their contents follows this introduction. Each unit is based on a theme that we intuitively feel is the basis of many adult conversations. Within each unit there are at least three related topics chosen to appeal to adults. The units involve a mixture of different ways of working to provide variety and interest, and adaptation to the particular circumstances of a class is possible and desirable. There is no need to do all the tasks in a unit and teachers are encouraged to select tasks on the basis of content interest as well as relevance to the learners' perceived objectives. The earlier units are less demanding than the later ones as they concentrate on the learners' own experiences.

Some of the tasks are based on short listening inputs and these are on an accompanying cassette. The transcripts are on pages 64–66. The talks and stories could be read by the teacher if a tape-recorder were unavailable. The book also contains three projects (pages 54–56) designed to help learners use English inside and outside the classroom. In each project the group is asked to work as a team and organize an out-of-class activity. The projects are optional but they encourage collaboration and give practice in taking part in meetings.

Another feature of the book is feedback tasks (pages 57–63) on important areas of oral performance such as hesitation devices, fillers, weaknesses in the use of tenses, etc. They are designed to be used on sections of students' recorded discussions or individual presentations and will allow you to assess individual progress as well as identifying areas of difficulty for further practice. In a small class it is worth going through the recorded material on an individual/small group basis. In a larger class the teacher could focus on examples of general interest. Keep some of the early recordings so that students can listen to their progress.

Using the materials

If learners are unfamiliar with task-based fluency material they will have to be prepared for it. As learning is a habit this can take time, and confidence in the value of such tasks is a crucial factor. Preparation should cover the 'how' and 'why'. The 'why' involves an appeal to the learners' common sense. There should also be constant reference to the way in which individual tasks contribute to the overall aim of the book. It helps learners improve their performance if they know what they are getting from specific tasks.

Learners may also need guidance in how to take part. This involves the gradual introduction of techniques in order to proceed from the known to the unknown. For example, learners used to very controlled oral work will need to be introduced to pairwork before approaching this material. Learners who are used to highly-structured pair and group work may find the material threatening because of the amount of freedom involved. The rule is not to ask them to do too much too soon by shortening the practice asked of them and monitoring each stage carefully. In the early stages they may also need considerable help with the instructions so always check they understand by asking for a demonstration or other evidence that they know what to do.

Fluency materials can be used successfully with monolingual classes even though learners may find themselves using the mother tongue. This is valid if it is with a view to understanding the input and/or producing the output they want by way of collaboration, although it is ideal if they are prepared to use English only. The following strategies may help:

- praise learners who speak in English
- prove to learners that they can use English by getting them to reflect on and discuss what they use the mother tongue for
- monitor how the tasks are going but do not correct learners as they are working so that they can concentrate on what they want to say.

The main preparation which is required in using this material is to think through what the tasks will mean in terms of the organization of the classroom so that discussion is facilitated and learners can be helped to move quickly and efficiently into and out of groups. After a while these procedures will become established and a sure sign of success is when the teacher is barely noticed for an entire lesson. However the learners should never feel you are doing nothing and the teacher should be able to give help with vocabulary and other problems. (It is therefore important to take up a position where it is easy to attract your attention.) At the same time you should avoid taking part except as a genuine participant and use any time available to quietly monitor and assess with a view to organizing feedback and planning future input.

The management of time is also very important. Activities should never be allowed to drag on but, at the same time, rapid completion of one task after another is usually a sign that something is wrong. Obviously each class will work at a slightly different rate and some tasks may be more engaging than others.

CHECKLIST

UNIT	SECTION	AIMS TO:	STUDENT ACTIVITIES	TIMING
1 PEOPLE pages 2–7	**1** What sort of person are you?	help learners get to know each other	choosing pictures; questionnaire; small group discussion	30–40 min
	2 Family life	help learners talk about the family; get to know each other	table completion; pair work; mingling; class discussion	40 min
	3 They remind me of . . .	practise talking about people	personal response to photos; vocabulary exercise in pairs; class follow-up	30–40 min
2 EXPERIENCE pages 8–13	**1** Sharing experiences	talk about personal experiences	mingling; listening; sharing	minimum of 20 min per task over 2 or 3 lessons
	2 A good experience?	analyse and discuss a problem; establish priorities	pair and group response to text and stimulus material	40–50 min
	3 A new sport?	discuss, research & report back on dangerous sports	vocabulary building; mingling; listening to information; asking questions	2 lessons 20 min & 40 min
3 TIME pages 14–19	**1** Changes over time	give an opinion on whether people change	reading and discussion in pairs; exchange of personal information; group discussion	50–60 min
	2 Time is money	discuss robots and work together on a problem	identify and discuss uses of robots; design & present a proposal; sketch & display	40 min Task 1–3 Task 4, 15 min
	3 Stories for our time	practise telling a story	read, listen to & exchange stories in pairs & groups; group story preparation	60 min

UNIT	SECTION	AIMS TO:	STUDENT ACTIVITIES	TIMING
4 ACHIEVEMENTS pages 20–25	1 Historical achievements	practise presenting factual information	listening prior to preparing talk on history; pair/group & individual work/ presentation	80 min over 2 lessons
	2 The Guinness Book Of Records	practise seeking & giving opinion	respond to stimulus material	2 separate 20 min
	3 Success	practise reasoned argument; story telling	reflection; vocabulary building and experience exchange; group story preparation & presentation	80 min
5 PLEASURE pages 26–33	1 Holidays	develop personal enquiry & exchange	pair work and mingling; questioning & planning	20 min
	2 Food	develop ability to work together	creative problem solving; questionnaire completion & analysis; discussing results	Task 1, 20 min 40 min rest
	3 The pleasures of life—British style	introduce a cross cultural dimension	pair and group discussion; optional interviews	20 min
	4 The pleasures of life—Japanese style	further cross cultural discussion	listening and group discussion; group discussion	30–40 min 20 min

UNIT	SECTION	AIMS TO:	STUDENT ACTIVITIES	TIMING
8 BEHAVIOUR pages 48–53	**1** Problems at work	analyse a human problem to work out solutions	reading and discussion of case; pair, group and class evaluation of solutions	40 min
	2 The natural way	give opportunity to discuss social phenomena	diagrams and captions as stimulus to discussion	40 min
	3 Competitiveness	stimulate thought on how to improve as language learners	questionnaire as basis for discussion in groups/class	40 min

1 People

1 What sort of person are you?

Task 1

Your holidays show what you are really like.
Look at the pictures. Which would you choose for a holiday?

The family house

A resort

Somewhere exotic

Sites and monuments

Local entertainment

Sun, sea and sand

Now find out the names of other people in your class who have chosen the same picture. Do you have other things in common? Ask about their interests, hobbies, age, family, marital status, etc.

Task 2

Complete the questionnaire about holidays. Work on your own. Your answers will show what kind of person you really are.

1   When I'm on holiday I usually:
   a   go to the family house.
   b   go camping in a quiet place.
   c   go to a popular holiday resort in my own country.
   d   try to visit a foreign country.
   e   look for sun, sea and sand; it doesn't matter where.

2   I like being anywhere where there:
   a   are exotic and different things and I can be with the local people.
   b   are very few people and I can be on my own.
   c   are lots of historical sites and monuments.
   d   are lots of sporting activities.

3 In the evenings I usually:
   a go to the clubs and discos.
   b try to find where the local people spend their evenings and go there.
   c have a quiet meal and go to bed early.
   d try a different restaurant every night.

5 Before my holiday I usually:
   a read as much as possible about the place I'm going to.
   b try to learn a little of the language if I'm going to a foreign country.
   c do nothing in the way of preparation.
   d buy lots of new clothes and/or visit a solarium.

4 I like going on holiday:
   a with a group of friends.
   b alone.
   c with my partner.
   d with my family.

6 During the holiday I:
   a send postcards to everyone.
   b never send any postcards at all.
   c prefer to telephone my friends and family.
   d write long letters to the people I feel close to.

Task 3

Form a group. Look at page 67 to find out what kind of person you are. Compare your results with other people in the group. Talk to someone who had similar results and to someone who had different results. Do you have similar personalities or not?

Task 4

Choose two people in your group who had different results. Which of these adjectives apply to yourself and to the others when you are on holiday?

energetic   solitary   relaxed   fun-loving sociable noisy
lazy   unsociable adventurous curious   quiet   independent

Use a dictionary or ask your teacher or another student for help if necessary.

Are you the same in class?

Task 5

Listen to extract 1 on the cassette. Lucy is talking to John about his holiday. Listen for expressions that Lucy uses to encourage John to continue speaking, e.g. *Oh, and how did you find it this time?*

Practise how you would say these. Ask your teacher to help you with the intonation.

Task 6

In groups of four, find out about each other by asking questions about people's holidays. Encourage people to say as much as possible. If you have a cassette recorder, record about two minutes of your conversation. Did you sound interesting and encouraging? Keep this recording until the end of the course.

2   Family life

Task 1

- Who does the cleaning in your family?
- Who does the cooking?
- Who looks after the money?

Complete the table below.

Activity	*Person responsible*
shopping for food	
cooking	
cleaning	
gardening	
repairs	
decorating	
looking after money	
looking after children	
packing for holidays	

Now find out how the other students answered the same questions. You have a maximum of five minutes to find the names of learners who have similar family responsibilities to you.

Task 2

Work with a partner. You want to find out about someone's family. Write down as many questions as you can think of to ask. When you have finished decide which questions can go in each column.

Questions you can ask a stranger you have just met	*Questions you can ask someone you know well*

Task 3

In groups of four exchange information about your family. Talk about:

- the size of your family (include uncles, aunts, cousins, etc.)
- where most of your family live — in the same house/town/in different parts of the country
- how often they meet — where? when?

Remember to encourage people when they are speaking. Listen, show interest and ask them questions. Try to complete the chart while people are talking.

	FAMILY			
	1	**2**	**3**	**4**
Size				
Do they live in the same house/town?				
When they meet				
Where they meet				
Other interesting information				

What are the main similarities and differences between your group's families? Choose someone to report your observations to the whole class.

Make statements like:
Most of the people in our group have a large family.
Most people's families don't live in the same town.

When you have heard all the reports, decide on one of these statements as a summary of your discussion.

- Family life is very similar wherever you are.
- Family life varies greatly.

3   They remind me of . . .

Task 1

Look at the photographs below and on the opposite page. Do they
remind you of anyone? Why?
In pairs, tell each other about the people the pictures remind you of.

a

b

c

d

e

f

g   h   i

Task 2

Which of these words describe any of the people in the photographs.

sexy	athletic	warm	friendly
cute	fascinating	silly	aggressive
trendy	old-fashioned	boring	affluent
smart	poor	wise	patient
ambitious	amusing	mischievous	dependable

Look up the words in a dictionary or ask your teacher to help you.

Task 3

Tell the class about the words you chose and see if they agree. Ask your teacher to help you find other words if you need them.

2
Experience

1 Sharing experiences

Task 1

Take a large sheet of paper and write down the following:

a three places
- a place you have been on holiday
- a place that is important to you
- a place where you like to be alone

b three years/dates
- the year that changed you most
- the year you were happiest
- the year you first went to school

c three people
- someone you will never forget
- someone you like a lot
- someone you don't like very much

d three memories
- a happy memory
- a sad memory
- your earliest memory

When you have done this find someone in your class who you do not know very well. Sit together, exchange sheets and ask each other questions about the information on your new sheet, for example:

What happened in 19 . . . ?　　*Tell me about . . .*
Why do you like . . . ?　　*Why do you like going to . . . ?*

Find out as much as possible about any of the statements that interest you.

Task 2

After about 10 minutes take your own piece of paper back and do the same thing with another student. Finally, as a group, share some of the most interesting things you have learnt about the people you have spoken to.

Task 3

Listen to extract 2 on the cassette. A man is telling his friends about an embarrassing moment. Look at these questions before you listen to his story.

1 Where does the story take place?
2 Who was there?
3 Why was it an embarrassing moment?

Listen to the extract again.

1 Put these events in the correct order.

The man bought something. ☐

He lost the top button from his trousers. ☐

He put both hands in his pockets.	☐
He left the shop quickly.	☐
He took the money out of his pocket.	☐

2 Decide if these statements are true or false. Give reasons for your answers.

	TRUE	FALSE
The man hid.	☐	☐
He pulled his zip up with one hand.	☐	☐
He left without paying.	☐	☐
He took both hands out of his pockets.	☐	☐
The woman tried not to look at him.	☐	☐

Task 4

Look at the feedback task on page 57. Listen to the extract again and see how the man keeps talking!

Task 5

Has anything similar happened to you before? Tell the other students about your most embarrassing moment.

Task 6

Sometimes we all have to do things we don't like! Look at the list of activities and choose the one that you dislike most.

- starting a new job
- taking an examination
- being interviewed for a new job
- travelling by plane
- going to live in a new country
- complaining in a shop or restaurant
- speaking in public
- giving someone bad news
- entering a room full of strange people
- going to the dentist's

Sit with a student who has chosen the same activity as you. Make a list of the aspects of the activity that you dislike most, e.g. waiting at airports when a plane is late. Join with another pair and share your lists. See if you can work out six pieces of advice that you would give to someone to help them get through the activity as easily as possible.

Share your ideas with the rest of the class and see if they have any other suggestions.

2   A good experience?

Task 1

Read this text which describes the dilemma of a young English girl.

Project Trust, a charity which aims to help people who are starving, has asked for young volunteers to work in Africa. Anna Smithson is 18 and has just left school. Her parents want her to go on to university, but Anna feels it would be a good experience to see something of the world first. She has never been away from home before and she thinks that adapting to a foreign country and helping people less fortunate than herself will give her a more balanced view of life. She has already been accepted as a volunteer, but her parents are very worried about her because the relief work she has been asked to help with is in a war zone and the living conditions there are very poor. Reports on the television show that people are often killed or taken prisoner and many simply die from one of the many diseases. They have told Anna that if she insists on going they will not pay any money to her while she is there and will not help her to go to university when she returns.

Discuss anything you do not understand in the text with a partner or ask your teacher for help. Try to work out the meaning of any new words by reading the text two or three times and thinking about the whole situation.

In pairs decide who is right — Anna or her parents. Give reasons for your decision.

Task 2

Look at these statements and decide whether you agree with them or not. Change the statements if you wish.

- Living in a strange environment is an important experience.
- A terrible or difficult experience helps to make you a better person.
- Children should obey their parents.
- Films and books are a substitute for personal experience.

Discuss your decisions with your partner. Do you want to change your opinions from Task 1 now that you have thought about these statements?

Join another pair and see if you have reached the same conclusions.

Task 3

These pictures show projects which young people in Britain have been involved in. The experiences offered by the projects include:

- sailing round the world with people from different countries
- taking physically-handicapped people on holiday so that they can see something beyond their own homes, and so that their families can have a rest
- raising money to help children in developing countries
- learning about nature and wildlife and helping to protect birds and animals in danger
- visiting lonely old people regularly and helping to decorate their homes.

Discuss these projects in groups of four and decide which offers the most experience of:

- working with other people
- other countries
- personal problems
- handling money
- helping others
- travel
- understanding other people's needs
- social problems
- a better understanding of the world we live in.

Task 4

When you have thought about each of the projects, work on an idea for a project of your own. Your aim should be to provide a useful project and as much good experience as possible with a minimum of cost. Choose one member of your group to present it to the class. When you do this, explain the sort of experience your project offers.

When all the groups have presented their projects vote for the best project.

3   A new sport?

Task 1

hang-gliding   sailing   motocross   waterskiing

wrestling   parascending   rock-climbing   pot-holing

windsurfing   surfing   horse riding   skiing

Look at the pictures and their captions and learn the English names for the activities.

Work with a partner if you want to and ask your teacher for help with pronunciation and stress.

Task 2

Work in groups of three or four.

Find out if anyone in your group has ever tried any of these activities.

Find out if anyone does them regularly.

Share your experiences and opinions of the sports. Do you like them?
Do you think they are safe? Would you like to try any of them? Why?

Discuss for about 10 minutes and ask one member of your group to
complete the table.

Activities someone has tried	*Activities someone wants to try*	*Activities we think are stupid and dangerous*

Choose one member of your group to report to the class.

Task 3

Ask your teacher to write on the blackboard all the activities that
people in the class want to try.

Find one or two students in the class who know something (or are
willing to find out) about each activity. Ask them to prepare a talk for
the next lesson.

In the next lesson the 'experts' on the sports should each set up an
information stand to present their sport. They can bring pictures and
equipment to the lesson, if possible. Students in the class can then
visit the stands and ask for information on the sport(s) they want to
try. Questions they could ask include:

Do you need lessons?   *How long does it take to learn?*
What equipment do I need?   *Where can you do the sport?*
Is it dangerous?   *How much does it cost?*

At the end of the lesson find out which students would still like to try
the sport and which ones have changed their minds. Ask them for
their reasons.

Task 4

Find out if a group of you who are interested in the same sport can go
and try it locally. Then tell the class about your experience in the
next lesson — in English, of course!

3

Time

1 Changes over time

Task 1

As we get older we change. Or do we?

Read this story and discuss anything you find difficult with a partner. Do not ask your teacher or look in a dictionary until you have read the story at least two or three times.

THE GIRL CAN'T HELP IT

Madonna was the sensation of 1984/5. Some said she was beautiful, others thought she was a mess. Her records and concerts attracted millions of fans.

In 1983 Madonna was nobody and she even tried to attract attention to herself by appearing in New York bars in her underwear. Then suddenly her first record album sold four million copies and Madonna was a star. She attracts a lot of attention both on and off the stage but, interestingly enough, she has been like this from an early age.

She was the daughter of a Chrysler car worker and her mother died of cancer when Madonna was only six years old. The little girl had to try hard to get noticed — because she was one of seven brothers and sisters who were moved from one relative to another in the Detroit area. In a family that size she found it hard to get her share of love and affection.

She felt so little love was directed towards her that she had to do everything she could to stand out. In an interview she said, 'I was so desperate I would even hurt myself, like burn my fingers deliberately, just to get attention. At family gatherings I'd climb on the table and start dancing. If I didn't get attention that way, then I'd make even more noise until I did.'

Discuss these questions with your partner.

- Have you ever heard of Madonna?
- What do you think of her?
- Do you think she is typical of most pop stars? Why?
- Do you think that most pop stars wanted attention as children? Which ones in particular? Why?
- On the basis of what you have read do you think people change as they get older?

Task 2

Now see how much you have changed by completing the table below.

Think back to your childhood and write down in the first column what was your favourite food, hobby, sport, etc. In the second column write down what you like most today.

Favourite	*As a child*	*Today*
Holiday		
Time of year		
Time of day		
Hobby		
Food		
Sport		
Place		
TV programme		
Type of book		
Person		

Task 3

Give your completed table to a partner. Take it in turns to ask each other questions about what you have written down.

Do this for about 5 minutes then write down:

- three important areas in which you think your partner has changed
- three important areas in which you think he/she has stayed the same.

Exchange what you have written with your partner and see if you agree with one another. Tell each other in what ways you think you have changed or not.

If you disagree with what your partner has written, explain why.

Task 4

Join other pairs to make a group of six. Which of these statements do you agree with? Use the results of Tasks 1–3 to give reasons for your answers.

- People never really change.
- There is something of the child in every person.
- Most of us improve when we get older.

Choose one person in your group to report your conclusions to the class.

2   Time is money

Task 1

These photographs show some examples of robots and their uses. In pairs, match the captions with the photographs.

1 *A robot playing basketball*
2 *A robot bomb investigation unit*
3 *A robot musician*
4 *A robot at work in a car factory*

Task 2

Look at the questions and note down a few ideas for use in a discussion.

- Are robots used in industry in your country? Why? Why not?
- What are robots used for?
- Can robots do a better job than people? Give examples.
- Do you think robots are a good idea when there is a lot of unemployment?
- Should robots be introduced everywhere in the world? Think of some of the arguments for and against this idea.
- What can we do with the time we save?

When you are ready, sit in a circle with four or five other students. If possible, record what the group says. Now discuss this quotation.

'Technology made large populations possible; large populations make technology indispensable'

Joseph Wood Krutch *Penguin Dictionary of Quotations*

Task 3

Work in groups of four to six students. You are a group of consultants. Your client is a firm that makes robots and it would like your opinion on whether or not it should produce an advanced robot 'housewife'.

Assume that the average wage a housewife can earn outside the home is £10 per hour. Your task is to work out how much time and money you could save by using a robot. The average British housewife is estimated to work 77 hours per week. Prepare a report for the class under the headings:

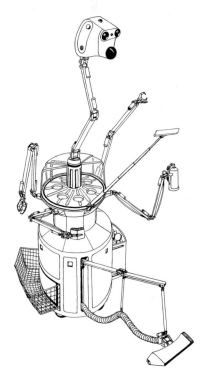

- Activities that a housewife is usually involved in, e.g. cleaning the house.
- Activities a robot could take over.
- Cost of the robot.
- Savings that would be made as the result of introducing the robot.
- The advantages and disadvantages of a robot doing the housewife's job.
- Recommendations for your client.

Task 4

Robots could save us time and money in other areas. In addition to a robot housewife we could have a robot traffic warden or police officer, a robot waiter or even a robot secretary.

Decide on an application for a robot and, working in pairs, sketch out your design. When you have finished, put your sketch up on the wall of the classroom and explain it to other students.

3   Stories for our time

Task 1

Read this story.

THE LITTLE GIRL AND THE WOLF

One afternoon a big wolf waited in a dark forest for a little girl to come along carrying a basket of food to her grandmother. Finally a little girl did come along and she was carrying a basket of food. "Are you carrying that basket to your grandmother?" asked the wolf. The little girl said yes, she was. So the wolf asked her where her grandmother lived and the little girl told him and he disappeared into the wood.

When the little girl opened the door of her grandmother's house she saw that there was somebody in bed with a nightcap and nightgown on. She had approached no nearer than twenty-five feet from the bed when she saw that it was not her grandmother but the wolf, for even in a nightcap a wolf does not look any more like your grandmother than the Metro-Goldwyn lion looks like Calvin Coolidge. So the little girl took an automatic out of her basket and shot the wolf dead.

Moral: It is not so easy to fool little girls nowadays as it used to be.

Fables for our Time James Thurber

Discuss anything you find difficult in the story with a partner.

Do not look in a dictionary or ask your teacher for help until you have read the story at least two or three times.

Task 2

Work in groups of three or four.

Does anyone know the traditional story on which this story is based? What is it called?

Can you tell the traditional version of the story? Help each other to do so.

Now listen to extract 3 on the cassette. You will hear someone telling the traditional version of the same story. Listen carefully and see how well you did.

Is there a similar story in your country? How does it differ from the one you have just heard?

Task 3

Look at the illustrations of some traditional stories. Do you know
what the stories are? Do they remind you of any stories in your own
country? Tell your partner about them.

Task 4

The Little Girl and the Wolf was written by an American novelist
called James Thurber. In 1940 he published a collection called *Fables
for our Time*. Thurber's idea was to use stories which were very
similar to traditional ones to comment on American society.

In groups of four make up a modern version of a traditional story.
Start by trying to find a story that you are all familiar with. Ask your
teacher for help if necessary.

Work to produce a modern version of the story and then practise
telling it. Listen to extract 3 on the cassette again if you want to and
try to copy some of the intonation and phrases useful for story-
telling. If possible get one member of your group to record the story.

4 Achievements

1 Historical achievements

Task 1

Look at this photograph of Machu Picchu

In pairs work out some possible answers to the questions.

- Who do you think built the city?
- Where do you think it was built?
- When do you think it was built?

Tell each other anything else you know about the city and the part of the world you think it is in.

Task 2

You are going to hear a short talk about Machu Picchu. Before you listen decide with your partner whether you think these statements are true or false.

- Machu Picchu was built before Columbus discovered the Americas.
- The city was built without the use of the wheel.
- The natives used to grow potatoes and maize.
- The natives were unable to read and write.
- Machu Picchu was part of a great empire that lasted for centuries.

Task 3

Now listen to extract 4 on the cassette and see how many of your decisions about Machu Picchu were right.

Was there any information that surprised you? If so, tell the class about it.

Task 4

Work alone and spend some time finding out as much as you can about your country at the beginning of the sixteenth century. Prepare a short talk to present to a group of other students.

Try to include answers to the following questions:

- What was happening in your country at the time Machu Picchu was built?
- Was it part of an empire?
- Were any famous buildings built at that time?
- What did the people do for a living?
- Could they read and write?
- Did they have transport?
- Who was their leader?

If all the students in the class are from the same country, choose different towns or different periods of history to give some variety to the task.

Task 5

In groups of four, take it in turn to give your talks. When you are listening to the others, try to ask questions which show you are interested in what they are saying.

2   The Guinness Book of Records

Task 1

The Guinness Book of Records is published each year and lists all the known records and achievements in the world, e.g. the biggest family, the oldest person, the fastest mile run by a man/woman, the highest mountain, etc. It also records some achievements which are not so well known. Here are some of the achievements from *The Guinness Book of Records* for 1985.

Bubble-gum blowing
The greatest reported diameter for a bubble-gum bubble is 48.9 cm by Susan Montgomery, 18, of Fresno, California in April 1979.

Hula hooping
The longest recorded marathon for a single hoop is 72 hours by Kym Coberly in Denton, Texas on 17–20 October 1984.

Coin balancing
Bruce McConachy raised the record to 200 Canadian cent coins balanced on a vertical free-standing commemorative $10 coin at West Vancouver, Canada on 8 February 1984.

House of cards
Anthony de Bruxelles achieved 62 storeys in Weinheim, West Germany on 4–6 May 1984

Grape catching
The greatest distance at which a grape thrown from level ground has been caught in the mouth is 82.4 metres by Paul J. Taville, at Dedham, Massachusetts, USA on 9 August 1979.

Milk bottle balancing
The greatest distance walked by a person continuously balancing a full milk bottle on the head is 38.6 kilometres by Ashita Furamn of Jamaica, New York, USA.

Eating
1 kilogram of snails was eaten in 3 minutes 45.78 seconds in Hever Castle, Kent on 27th June 1984. Name not given.

Thirty-eight soft-boiled eggs were eaten in 75 seconds by Peter Dowdeswell at Kilmarnock Carnival on 28 May 1984.

In groups of three or four students, discuss your reactions to these records.

Do people try for similar records in your country?

Tell the others in your group about any you have seen, heard of or taken part in.

Why do you think that people try to get into *The Guinness Book of Records*? Would you? Why? Why not?

Task 2

The Guinness Book of Records also records more serious achievements. Even in the twentieth century, when the world seems much smaller and it is difficult to imagine new things to discover or to do for the first time, people are still looking to be the first, to achieve something great.

Look at these photographs of famous achievements.

First circumnavigation of the poles — Trans Globe Expedition

First conquest of Everest — Sir Edmund Hilary and Tenzing

First four minute mile — Roger Bannister

First heart transplant — Christian Barnard

First walk on the moon — Neil Armstrong

First direct flight across the Atlantic—Alcock and Brown

Work with a partner and decide which of the above achievements was:

- the most dangerous
- the most beneficial to man
- the least beneficial to man
- the most difficult
- the biggest waste of money.

When you have decided, join another pair and compare your ideas.

3 Success

Task 1

Some famous people have been talking about why and how they became successful in *Tactics, The Art and Science of Success* by Edward de Bono. Here are some of the quotations from the book. Read them and discuss their meanings with a partner.

'I remember dreaming that maybe one day I would be famous.'

Jackie Stewart, Formula 1 World Champion Racing Driver

'People who are just in it for money — they usually fail.'

Robert Holmes à Court, Multimillionaire businessman

'If somebody said to me, "Look I'll offer you a lousy job but you'll get paid £3 million pounds a year," I'd say, "Thank you very much, no." '

Charles Williams CBE, Managing Director of Henry Ansbacher & Co. a London Merchant Bank

'Self-image is all important.'

Charles Williams CBE, Managing Director of Henry Ansbacher & Co., a London Merchant Bank

'I was always told (as a child) that doing something well was just a matter of trying hard enough.'

Jeane Kirkpatrick, US Ambassador to the UN

'My voice is not something that I have ever developed or had trained. Yet some people would regard me as one of the best exponents of a particular style in the country.'

Sting, pop singer

Ask your teacher for help if you find any of them difficult to understand.

Task 2

Here are some words and phrases that people often use when they are talking about why people are successful. Make sure you know what each one means. Work with a partner and use a dictionary or ask your teacher for help.

hard work	being in the right place at the right time
energy	knowing the right people
money	talent
luck	publicity
ambition	organization
determination	courage

Are there any other factors not listed here which you think are also important to success? If so, find the words in English and add them to the list.

Task 3

In pairs look again at the quotations in Task 1 and decide which of the
words and phrases were important for each person.

Task 4

Which of the factors in Task 2 do you think are most important for
success?

Now think of someone who you think has been very successful.
(It does not need to be someone famous, but it could be.)

Spend 5 minutes planning how you would tell his/her success story,
showing how the factors that you think are important helped.

When you are ready, sit with a partner and tell each other the
success story you have prepared.

Task 5

In groups of five or six talk about your own responses to this
question.

> DO YOU REALLY WANT TO BE SUCCESSFUL?

What does the group think are the most important advantages and
disadvantages of being successful. Choose one person from your
group to report your conclusions to the class.

Task 6

In 1981 *Rags to Riches* was a best-selling novel and also a TV serial.
People like reading stories about someone who starts life poor and at
a disadvantage and eventually becomes rich, or successful or famous
(or even better all three!).

Perhaps it is because they hope the same thing could happen to
them.

In groups of four make up your own best-selling success story. You
must try to use all the words and phrases below somewhere in your
story!

adventurous	lipstick	an only child
sexy	windsurfing	seriously ill
an aggressive man	charity	guitar
miserable	generous	earliest memory
lonely	a romantic look	looking after children

Tell your story to the rest of the class. When you have heard all the
stories, vote for the one that will be the best-seller!

5

Pleasure

Group A

Group B

1 Holidays

Task 1

Look at the photographs. Which ones show what you like on holiday?
Choose one photograph from each group. Do not tell anyone which
ones you have chosen.

Group C

Task 2

Go around the class and, by asking questions, try to find someone who has chosen exactly the same three pictures as you.

When you have found someone, tell each other your reasons for choosing the pictures.

Now plan a holiday together. Agree on:

- where you will go
- when you will go
- where you will stay
- how you will travel
- what you would like to do when you get there.

Task 3

When you have decided on your holiday, go round the class again and see, if by asking questions, you can find another pair who have planned a similar holiday.

2 Food

Task 1

You arrive late at a friend's holiday house. All the shops are shut and you would like to make a nice meal for you and the person you are with. You are both very hungry. You look in the cupboard and in the fridge and you find:

a few onions and tomatoes	one chicken leg	a tin of tuna fish
a jar of strawberry jam	a tin of pineapple	a packet of rice
a tub of yoghurt (natural)	four potatoes	a tin of dried milk
a tin of baked beans	six eggs	five apples

The cupboard also contains basics such as salt, pepper, dried herbs and spices, oil and sugar.

In pairs, plan a meal for two which uses as many of the ingredients as possible. When you are ready, tell the class what you intend to make and be ready to explain how to make any of the dishes if necessary.

When you have heard everyone's menu decide as a class which one is the best.

Task 2

Is food one of the pleasures of life or not? Make two groups in the class — one made up of people who think food is a pleasure of life and the other made up of people who do not think much about food, are not particularly interested in preparing or eating it, and see it as a nuisance to have to stop and eat.

Complete the questionnaire individually.

EATING HABITS QUESTIONNAIRE

1   How much time do you spend in a normal week preparing meals?
 a   1 hour or less
 b   2–4 hours
 c   4–6 hours
 d   more than 6 hours

2   How much time do you spend eating in a normal week?
 a   less than 7 hours
 b   between 8 and 10 hours
 c   between 10 and 12 hours
 d   more than 12 hours

3   How many meals do you eat in a normal day?
 a   two or less
 b   three
 c   four
 d   more than four

4 Which of these do you eat more than four times a week (tick each one)?

  a tinned foods
  b frozen foods
  c fresh meat
  d fresh vegetables
  e fresh fruit
  f cakes and/or biscuits
  g fast food (e.g. MacDonald's hamburgers, etc.)
  h sweets and/or chocolate
  i nibbles (e.g. crisps, salted peanuts, snacks, etc.)
  j fresh fish
  k bread
  l cheese
  m eggs
  n nuts
  o pulses (e.g. lentils, dried beans, etc.)

Now put a cross (X) by the three that you think you eat most of in a week.

5 How often do you eat in restaurants?

  a less than once a week
  b 1–3 times a week
  c 4–6 times a week
  d more than 6 times a week

6 Who normally does the cooking for you at home?

  a I cook for myself.
  b my partner
  c my mother
  d a servant

Now compare your questionnaires within your group.

Task 3

Are there any general statements you can make about your group?

- Do you eat similar things?
- Do you all cook?

Prepare a short report on your group's eating habits and choose one person in the group to present it to the rest of the class.

Task 4

When you have heard the reports from both groups, work as a class and answer these questions:

- Were there any big differences between the two groups? What were they?
- Did you find any of the results surprising? Why?

3   The pleasures of life — British style

Task 1

Many British people would list one or more of the following as being a pleasure in life.

- a cup of tea in bed
- walking the dog
- having a pint (of beer) in the local (pub)
- afternoon tea at 5 p.m.
- doing the garden
- reading the Sunday newspaper
- DIY (this stands for Do It Yourself, which means making your own furniture, home improvements, decorating, etc.)
- Sunday afternoon walks
- Sunday lunch with the family
- going for a drive in the country
- sitting in the local park
- a good book

Task 2

In groups of four decide which of these you also think is a pleasure.
Which ones do you find strange? Why?
What other things would you add to the list yourself?

Task 3

Find another student who comes from the same country or work
alone.

List five things that you think people in your country consider to be
pleasures in life.

Compare your list to that of students from another country and to the
list in Task 1. What are the similarities and differences? Do you think
the British are different from other nationalities?

Task 4

Try to interview as many British or American people as possible
about what they see as their pleasures in life. Report back to the
class in the next lesson.

4   The pleasures of life — Japanese style

One of life's pleasures is a bath. For many people having a bath is more than just a way of keeping clean. For the Romans the baths were a place to meet, to discuss business and above all to relax. In many parts of the world, even today, the bath is still a social event.

Task 1

Listen to extract 5 on the cassette entitled *The Japanese Way of Bathing.*

Task 2

Now look at these questions before listening to the extract again.

- Where do the Japanese relax when they are on holiday?
- What do you have to do *before* you get into a bath in Japan?
- What are some of the advantages of a Japanese bath?

Task 3

Imagine you are a tourist guide in Japan. What instructions would you give to a new arrival about the Japanese way of bathing?

Task 4

Look at the pictures below.

Discuss these questions in groups of four.

- Have you experienced any of these baths? Tell the others about them if you have.
- What happens in your country? Are there any special procedures for bathing?
- Is there a public bath where people can go to meet and relax?
- Do men and women go together?
- When you wash do you prefer a bath or a shower?

Task 5

In groups, look at these photographs of Japanese pastimes.

a   b   c

Match these captions to the photographs.

1 Kabuki theatre
2 A tea ceremony
3 Sumo wrestling

Write down what you know about these pastimes.

Write down the questions you would want to ask to find out more about them.

See if anyone in the class can answer your questions.

Now read the notes on page 67. Have you discovered anything new? These traditional pastimes are still very popular in Japan today. Do you know of any traditional pastimes from another country? Tell the other students about them. In what ways are they different from the Japanese pastimes in this unit? In what ways are they the same?

6

Money

1 Bingo!

Newspaper bingo, in which people have to match numbers published in a newspaper with those on cards delivered to their homes, is the latest way of winning large sums of money in Britain and prizes can be as much as one million pounds! The game was introduced to help sell more newspapers and some people now only buy the paper to see if they have won. Even *The Times* has its own version of the game which is based on the stock exchange!

Task 1

Answer the questions in small groups. Ask your teacher for help if necessary.

- Is newspaper bingo still played in Britain?
- Which papers offer it?
- Do you know what the 'football pools' are? How do they work?
- Do you have any similar games in your country? What are they?
- What other opportunities are there for you to win lots of money in your country?
- Some people say that these games are a British disease. Do you agree?
- Would you try newspaper bingo if you could? Why?

Task 2

Look at this advertisement for a British football pools firm.

And the best thing is—it can happen to you. The lifestyle of thousands of people in Britain today has changed beyond their wildest dreams due to a win on the Pools.
People just like Marion Smith . . .

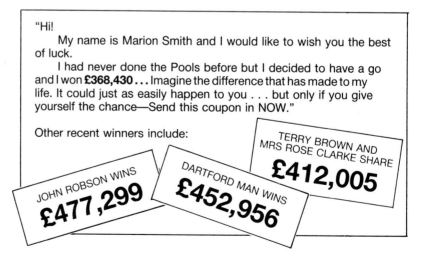

"Hi!
    My name is Marion Smith and I would like to wish you the best of luck.
    I had never done the Pools before but I decided to have a go and I won **£368,430 . . .** Imagine the difference that has made to my life. It could just as easily happen to you . . . but only if you give yourself the chance—Send this coupon in NOW."

Other recent winners include:

JOHN ROBSON WINS **£477,299**

DARTFORD MAN WINS **£452,956**

TERRY BROWN AND MRS ROSE CLARKE SHARE **£412,005**

Obviously winning a large sum of money does 'make a difference to your life'. In pairs, discuss what sort of difference.

Task 3

Read what happened to some big winners.

Donald and Ruth Williams won one million pounds from *The Sun*. Donald was a businessman who was divorced from his first wife and had just married Ruth. When they won:

- They bought a seventeenth-century mansion outside Bristol.
- They flew to the United States on Concorde for a holiday.
- They exchanged their BMW for a Rolls Royce.
- Donald gave up a successful sign-making business.

They are now looking for a new business.

June Walsh won one million pounds from the *Daily Mirror*. She was a cleaning lady with five daughters. When she won:

- She moved from a £15 a week rented bungalow into her own bungalow.
- She set up investments for her family with the help of a solicitor and a tax expert.
- She bought a new bed and a remote control TV. (She still cannot operate it!)
- She has retired quietly.

Father Dominic Ryan, a 65-year-old Catholic priest, won £109,000 on the football pools 14 years ago.

- He bought himself a new Mini.
- He gave all the remaining money to church repairs, to an orphans' home, to Bangladesh flood relief and to victims of the 1971 Glasgow Ibrox Park soccer tragedy. (A stand in the football stadium collapsed killing and injuring a large number of people.)

He said afterwards that writing the cheques to give the money away gave him a great deal of pleasure.

Eric and Mary Hope were the *Express* millionaires of the month. He was a 61-year-old motor mechanic and she was a 58-year-old grandmother. When they won:

- They moved out of their council house into a £40 a night hotel because they felt that others deserved the council house more.
- Eric gave up his job.

After a year they were still looking for a house, still driving the same 5-year-old car and were planning a holiday.

Look again at the different things that the winners did with their money. Is it possible to divide the list into categories? e.g. giving money to charity.

- Decide with your partner what the categories are.
- Decide which of these people you think made the best use of their money.

Compare your decisions with another pair's and see if you agree. Give reasons for your decisions if they are different.

Task 4

Imagine that you and three friends in your class have, as a group, just won £750,000 on the football pools. You have decided to have a meeting to help and advise each other on how best to share out and use the money.

Make a plan of how you personally think the money should be used. It could include:

- immediate personal needs
- ideas for investment
- donations to charity
- help for family and friends
- extravagances and luxuries.

Meet with the other three. Compare plans and try to reach some agreement.

2   Brother can you spare me ... ?

'Brother can you spare me a dime' is an expression which was used in the United States during the 1930s Depression. During that time many people were unemployed and very short of money. Sometimes when they saw an affluent-looking stranger they would go up to him and beg for a dime, which is 10 cents.

Task 1

Listen to extract 6 on the cassette. You will hear a woman talking about something that happened to her when she was abroad.

Read the questions then listen to the extract again and try to find the answers.

1   Where did the incident happen?
2   What did the man want?
3   What reasons did he give?
4   Why did the woman help him?
5   Why did she feel stupid and guilty by the end?

Task 2

Listen to the extract again and discuss the meaning of the following expressions in pairs. Ask your teacher for help if necessary.

1 'after checking into my hotel'
2 'window shopping and minding my own business'
3 'genuine and well-spoken'
4 'not being used to the money'
5 'a confidence trick'

Task 3

In a group of four, tell each other what you would have done in the same situation.

Has anything similar ever happened to you or to someone you know? Tell the others about it. Do your stories have anything in common?

Decide as a group what you think is the best way of dealing with such people.

Task 4

Imagine that you are in charge of a group of tourists in a town where there are a lot of confidence tricksters and beggars. In pairs, prepare a short talk (about 1 minute) to give to your tourists when they first arrive. Warn them about the situation and give them some advice on how to deal with it.

Do not frighten your clients or make them feel they have come to a dangerous or unpleasant place.

Be prepared to present your talk to the rest of the class if your teacher asks you to.

Task 5

In groups of four, decide on a 'hard-luck story' or a confidence trick which will get you a small sum of money from a stranger.

Try it on a member of another group or even on a teacher. Were you successful? If you were successful, save the money for Project 2!

3   Money for life!

Task 1

Work with a partner. Assume that you are a married couple without children. Decide how much you will have to spend on the following items if you are to have a good standard of living.

- Housing: e.g. 2 bedroomed flat
- Transport: e.g. 2 cars
- Holidays: e.g. a fortnight abroad in summer
- Entertainment: e.g. restaurant meals, theatre
- Food and drink: e.g. caviar and champagne
- Clothes: e.g. seasonal fashions
- Household goods: e.g. dishwasher

How much would you, as a couple, have to earn to pay for this standard of living, either in your own country or in England?

Task 2

Join another pair and compare your decisions. What were the similarities and differences in your conclusions? Agree on one version and present it to the class. Other students in the class may ask questions about your decisions.

Task 3

Complete the following table in groups of four.

THINGS WE HOPE WE CAN AFFORD IN 10 YEARS TIME

	Me	*Name:*	*Name:*	*Name:*
Housing				
Transport				
Holidays				
Entertainment				
Household goods				
Clothes				

Is this the same or different from what you can afford now? If the differences mean having a lot more money, how do you hope to get it?

Task 4

Below are some useful words and phrases for talking about money. Make sure you understand the meanings — ask a friend or your teacher for help, or use a dictionary. Then learn the words and phrases. Your teacher will help with pronunciation and stress.

a current account	an overdraft
a deposit account	a credit card
to pay interest (on)	a piggy bank
to make a profit	currency
high/low interest rates	to owe money
savings	a loan
investment	to pay cash
hire purchase	in debt
budget	to make a loss
borrow money	I can't afford it

Task 5

Most people have a time in their lives when they want to buy something special and expensive, or go on the holiday of a lifetime, or perhaps they just need to pay off an overdraft because they have already spent too much!

When this happens, most people need to save money, or at least spend less.

Think of a time when you had to save money or reduce your spending. Make a list of all the things you did to achieve your aim.

Share your ideas in groups of four. Who do you think was the most successful? Why?

7

Dreams

1 Dreams to remember

We all dream several times a night and yet we often remember nothing of what we dream. Why? There is no clear answer. Perhaps we do not remember dreams that occur when we are sleeping very deeply. Or perhaps Freud was right when he suggested that dreams are the fears and desires we repress or keep down when we are awake, and therefore we prefer to forget them.

Do you normally remember your dreams?

Some of the images that we often get when we dream include:

- cars
- doorways and staircases
- animals such as cats
- the sea

- mountains
- exotic faraway places
- childhood scenes
- a male or female figure.

Simulation Objective No. 3 by Rene Magritte (© DACS 1986)

Task 1

Close your eyes and try to bring back a recent dream. Try to remember as much detail as possible.

Open your eyes and walk around the class and ask other students about their dreams. Try to find someone who has similar dreams to you.

If you can't remember any dreams, try to find someone else who can't and discuss the reasons.

When you have finished, find out how many people in the class dream regularly about each of the things in the list. What other common images can you add to the list from talking to other students?

Task 2

Form a group of about five students and sit in a circle. Close your
eyes and concentrate. When one of you is ready, he/she should start
telling the others about a dream. (It can be real or imaginary.) Join in
and help to develop and extend the dream whenever you feel like it.

Task 3

Look at the picture. It is by the English poet William Blake
(1757–1827). Blake recorded some extremely frightening dreams.
Can you suggest an interpretation for Blake's dream?

Discuss your interpretation with a partner and then compare your
versions with the one on page 67.

2   The American dream

Task 1

Have you ever heard of the 'Great American Dream'? Work as a class and discuss what you understand by the expression. When you have compared your ideas look at page 68.

Task 2

Read the extract from *American Dreams Lost and Found* by Studs Terkel. A former Miss USA is talking about her experiences as a beauty queen.

Discuss anything you find difficult to understand with a partner. Do not ask your teacher for help or look in a dictionary until you have read the text at least twice.

I won the Miss USA pageant. I started to laugh. They tell me I'm the only beauty queen in history that didn't cry when she won. It was on network television. I said to myself: 'You're kidding.' Bob Barker, the host, said: 'No, I'm not kidding.' I didn't know what else to say at that moment. In the press releases, they call it the Great American Dream. There she is, Miss America, your ideal. Well, not my ideal, kid.

   The minute you're crowned you become their property and subject to whatever they tell you. They wake you up at seven o'clock next morning and make you put on a negligée and serve you breakfast in bed, so that all the New York papers can come in and take your picture sitting in bed, while you're absolutely bleary-eyed from the night before. They put on the Kayser-Roth negligée, hand you the tray, you take three bites. The photographers leave, you whip off the negligée, they take the breakfast away, and that's it. I never did get any breakfast that day. (Laughs)

Task 3

Discuss the following questions with your partner.

- Do you think she enjoyed her time as Miss USA?
- What do you think she particularly disliked?
- Do you think she was right? Would you feel the same?
- What do you think of beauty contests?
- Do they exist in your country?
- Would you let a member of your family enter one if you could do anything about it? Give reasons.
- Do you think that beauty contests are a good example of the Great American Dream?

Task 4

Continue to work with your partner. Tell each other about all the American influences that exist in your country. Make a list. Now decide which ones you think are good and which are bad. Give reasons.

What other American influences would you like to see in your country, if any?

Task 5

Join with another pair and share your ideas.

Would you like to go and live in America?

Discuss the advantages and disadvantages and report back to the class.

3   A dream society?

Task 1

Work in groups of five or six students.

Imagine that you have all gone to live on a 'dream island'. On this island you have everything you need to live quite well, food, water, housing, roads, transport, etc. All you need to do is decide how you are going to live peacefully together.

Look at the following statements. They could be the rules of your dream society.

- Nobody is allowed to own property.
- Everyone has total freedom to do whatever he/she wants.
- 'Love your neighbour.'
- Everyone will have the chance to do what he/she is interested in to help the group.
- The group will meet once a month to discuss problems.
- The group will have a leader elected by the others.
- Everyone in the group will be allowed to travel from the island whenever he/she wants.
- Nothing will be brought to the island without the agreement of the others.
- There will be a programme of sport, music and other entertainment for everyone.
- Women may have children but marriage to one partner is not allowed.

Do you agree with them?

Change any that you disagree with and add others if you wish.

Put the final list of rules in order of importance for keeping peace in the society. (The most important should be number 1 and so on.)

Task 2

When you have reached agreement on the list of rules, ask one member of your group to report to the class.

Discuss the similarities and differences between the groups' lists. Which list is the best?

Task 3

Look at this photograph.

Read and discuss the meaning of this poem in pairs.

Dreams

Hold fast to dreams
For if dreams die
Life is a broken-winged bird
That cannot fly.
Hold fast to dreams
For when dreams go
Life is a barren field
Frozen with snow.

Langston Hughes

This poem was published during the period the photograph was taken. Where and when was the photograph taken? Look at page 68 for information about the photograph, the poem and the poet.

What do you think the dreams of the people in the picture were? Do you think they were achieved? Why? Why not? Do you think that we should always dream of a better society?

4   How to achieve your dreams

Task 1

Most of us do not only dream at night. We have daydreams too.

In pairs, tell each other which of these things you can do and which ones you would like to be able to do well. Give reasons.

play the piano	yoga
play the guitar	landscape gardening
sing	play tennis
windsurf	play football
run a marathon	paint and draw
act	cook
design things	write

If you would like to do something else which is not in the list, tell your partner.

Task 2

Look at this list.

Determination	Courage	Patience
Energy	Stamina	Willpower
Ability	Practice	Qualifications
Time	Money	Motivation

Which of these are essential if you are to achieve your dreams?

Find out whether your partner thinks he/she will achieve his/her aim. If so, how? If not, why not?

Note down the reasons.

Task 3

In groups of four, use the answers you got in Task 1 to make lists
under the following headings:

Ways to achieve a personal dream	*Reasons for failure*

Now imagine that you are someone famous who has achieved a
personal dream. You have been asked to give a short talk (5 minutes)
to a group of young school-leavers. Give them advice on how to
succeed in their personal aims and how to make their dreams come
true.

In groups, prepare the talk using the information you have collected
to help you. Think about:

- things the young people should do if they hope to succeed
- things the young people should not do
- how to introduce the talk
- how to order the information
- how to end the talk.

Task 4

Choose one person in your group to present the talk to the rest of
the class. Practise giving the talk in your own group first and help the
speaker to improve his/her performance. Give the talk to the class
and record it if possible.

8

Behaviour

1 Problems at work

A lot of very different people come together at work and have to get on with one another. This can cause problems for many reasons and most people have experienced difficulties at work because someone is not behaving as he/she might.

Task 1

Read this account of a woman's problems at work. Discuss any difficulties you have in understanding it with a partner. Do not ask your teacher or look in a dictionary until you have read it at least twice.

Jean Anderson is 38. She is a very talented computer software specialist who started her own company at the age of 29. The company was successful, but in her early thirties Jean met and married a rich and successful solicitor and she gave up her career to have a child. Problems developed in her marriage and she got divorced when the child was 4 years old.

She had to go back to work in order to support herself and her daughter. Because she wanted security and felt she did not have the time to give to setting up her own business again, she took a job as a computer programmer with a large manufacturing firm. She became assistant to Bill Blows. Bill is 55 and was in the accounts department before the introduction of computers. He was made head of the computer section because of his long service with the firm and because he had a little experience of the type of work.

At first Jean and Bill got on very well together. However, after about 6 months she realized that there were a lot of weaknesses in the organization, that many of the projects she was working on needed changing and that most people in the department came to her when they wanted something, not to Bill. This meant a big increase in her workload. She talked to Bill and made some suggestions for improving things. At first he seemed interested and asked her to write them down, but after looking at them he said they were impractical and would not work. Jean's workload continued to increase and she became tense and upset. She wanted to leave the firm, but she had just bought a house and her daughter was happy in her new school. She decided that the answer was to avoid Bill as far as possible in future and only to do what she was specifically asked to do. After 11 months she took her annual holiday.

When she returned she found that her ideas for change had been implemented by Bill in her absence. She was about to go and speak to Bill when she received a note to go and discuss the possibility of a transfer to another branch of the firm in a different part of the country with the Personnel Manager. The reason given was her lack of co-operation with Bill Blows.

Task 2

What would you say to the Personnel Manager if you were Jean Anderson?

What do you think is the cause of her problem and what is the solution?

Task 3

In groups of four, take it in turn to present your solution to Jean's problem. Listen to the four solutions and then decide what are the advantages and disadvantages of each one, and what is the best course of action for her to take. Record your discussion if possible.

Include the things you have looked at in the feedback for earlier units, e.g. encouraging others to speak, building on what people say, etc. When you have time, compare this recording to the one you made in Unit 1. Listen for areas in which you have improved.

Task 4

Present the solution you have agreed on to the rest of the class. Note the similarities and differences in each group's solution.

2   The natural way

More and more people in the West are becoming interested in the
'natural' way of doing things, i.e. using only the things given to us by
nature rather than those made by man. People are questioning the
benefits of industrialization and, as a result, are changing the way
they behave. Medicine is no exception and an increasing number of
people are consulting 'alternative' doctors who do not believe in
manufactured drugs.

Task 1

Look at these pictures of 'natural' or 'alternative' medicine in pairs.
Which of the captions opposite goes with which picture?

Ask your teacher for help or use a dictionary if you cannot understand
the meaning of any of the words in the captions.

a

b

c

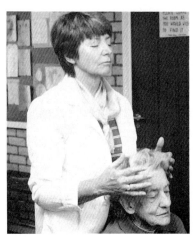

d

e

f

1 *Healing*   The use of one person's ability to heal another or cure disease by placing hands on the head, spine, or part where there is pain.

2 *Naturopathy*   The use of fasting, fruit and vegetable juices and natural foods to encourage the body's own healing powers; the idea being that illness comes from faulty living habits which lower the body's natural resistance to disease.

3 *Osteopathy*   The manipulation of parts of the body in the belief that mechanical faults in the body's structure are responsible for a lot of ill health. If normal movement is restored, then the nerves and blood supply can function properly and the patient's own healing processes will defeat the disease.

4 *Acupuncture*   The use of needles inserted in the skin to affect the flow of a 'vital energy' to help overcome pain or disease.

5 *Herbalism*   The use of plants as medicines.

6 *Homeopathy*   The use of a very small amount of a substance to cure symptoms which the substance would normally *cause* in a healthy person. For example a person with a sore throat would be given a cure made from something natural that would cause a similar problem in a healthy person.

Task 2

Check your answers to Task 1 with another pair. Then consider the following questions together.

- Have you ever heard of any of these forms of medicine?
- Have you or any of your friends ever tried one? What happened? Did they get better? Tell the others about it.
- Which of these practices do you believe in most? Why?
- Which practice would you avoid? Why?
- Would you consult an alternative doctor or not? Why?

Choose one member of your group to report your discussion to the rest of the class.

Task 3

Return to your groups of four and discuss the following.

In Britain and America recently there has been increasing interest in natural food, i.e. food which does not have added chemicals. Has this happened in your country? Have the majority of people changed their attitudes to what they are prepared to eat and drink? Do you think they should? What is your personal attitude to natural foods?

3   Competitiveness

Task 1

Do you think you are a competitive person?

☐ Yes
☐ No
☐ I haven't thought about it.

Do this questionnaire to find out. Work alone.

Here are some things that adult language learners tend to do when they are learning a foreign language. Tick the boxes which show how often you do the same things.

	Very often	*Quite often*	*Sometimes*	*Never*
1 I compare myself to other learners in the class.				
2 I compare my progress to what I expected before the start of the course.				
3 I feel hostile or aggressive towards other learners.				
4 I shout out answers; before other learners if possible.				
5 I compare my test results to those of other learners.				
6 I have experienced a wish to give up.				

Now get together with another student and discuss your answers.

Task 2

Join two other pairs and prepare a short summary of your questionnaire results. Make statements like:

All of us . . .
Only one of us . . .
Most of us . . .
None of us . . .

Present your results to the class.

Task 3

Consider these questions as a class:

- Did any of the results surprise you? Which ones? Why?
- What do the results tell you about your competitiveness?
- Do you think the group as a whole is more or less competitive than you thought?
- Are you more or less competitive in language learning than you think you are in life?

Task 4

Read this account and discuss any difficulties you have in understanding it with a partner. Do not ask your teacher for help or look in a dictionary until you have read the text at least twice.

Second language researchers who kept diaries of their own experiences in learning a second language found themselves exhibiting some or all of the behaviour described in the questionnaire. The conclusion of one of the researchers is that the learner sees himself as being either more or less successful than other language learners (or his own expectations). If he sees himself as successful then his learning is improved. If he does not see himself as successful then anxiety increases. This can either cause him to increase his effort to improve so that he feels he has to become better than other members of the class, i.e. he becomes more competitive, or, it can make him withdraw and decide to stop trying.

Task 5

Now discuss the following questions with the whole class.

- Do you agree with the researcher's conclusions?
- Can you suggest any ways in which the learners in your group can help each other and themselves?

PROJECTS

PROJECT 1: Planning a social event for the class

Aim

To organize a meal or party for all the members of the class.

Task

You are going to take part in a meeting. During the meeting you must decide on the following:

- a time for the party or meal
- a place where it can be held
- how much to spend.

Decide who will do each of the following jobs to prepare for the party or meal:

- collect the money and keep a record of what is spent
- prepare a menu
- shop for the food
- shop for the drinks
- make sure there are enough knives, forks, glasses, plates, etc.
- prepare and decorate the room
- give people a lift to and from the party
- lay the table
- organize the music
- organize the lighting
- clear up afterwards
- do the washing up.

You may be able to think of other jobs.

Preparation for the meeting

- Think of suggestions for the time, place, etc.
- Decide which of the jobs you think you can do well.
- Think which jobs other members of your class could do well.

The meeting

Decide who will be the chairperson. The chairperson's job is to make sure the meeting goes quickly and efficiently by asking for ideas and helping people to agree.

Decide who will be the secretary. The secretary's job is to write down any decisions and plans and the names of the people who agree to do each job.

The meeting should take 45 minutes and at the end everyone should know what he/she will do to help make the party a success. Ask your teacher to help by putting an agenda on the board before you start.

After the meeting

In the next few lessons ask your teacher for 5 minutes so that you can check how the plans and preparations for your party are going.

Of course, during the party you will all speak only English! Have a good time!

PROJECT 2: Raising money for charity

Aim

To raise a sum of money for a charity or charities you have decided upon.

Task

You are going to take part in a meeting. During the meeting you must decide on the following:

- a charity or charities that you want the money you raise to be sent to
- a plan for raising the money
- the approximate amount of money you would like to raise.

The only rule is that you should use as much English as possible.

Preparation for the meeting

Find examples of charities that you would like to support. Look in the newspaper, go to the library or ask your teacher for help if necessary.

Try to find out what the words below mean. They are all ways of raising money, which you might find useful.

- a lottery
- a raffle
- a sponsored walk/swim, etc.
- a collection
- a fund-raising event (e.g. a jumble sale)

Think of others.

The meeting

Decide on a chairperson and secretary as for Project 1. The meeting should take 45 minutes and at the end everyone should know how, where and when you are going to raise the money and which charity it will go to. Each person should also know exactly what he/she will do to help.

Good luck!

PROJECT 3: Making a radio programme

Aim

To organize the making of a radio programme which involves all the members of the class.

Task

You are going to take part in a meeting to plan the making of a radio programme. During the meeting you should decide on:

- the length of the programme
- the content of the programme, e.g. stories, interviews, talks, songs, announcements, advertisements, etc.
- who will do what to help make the programme
- a plan for the making of the programme.

Preparation for the meeting

Think of some ideas for the programme, e.g. possible stories, people to be interviewed.

Decide on a part of the programme you would be interested in helping to make.

NB   Some ideas for the programme could come from things you have done in other units and you could decide to include people outside your class.

The meeting

Decide on a chairperson and secretary for the meeting as for Projects 1 and 2.

The meeting should last 45 minutes and at the end you should have:

- an outline for the whole programme
- the names of students responsible for each of the parts and those responsible for equipment, production, etc.
- rehearsal times, when students will present their section of the programme to the class
- a recording plan.

Rehearsals

When each section is presented the class should decide on any changes and on the final order for recording.

The programme

When you have made your programme invite another class or another group of people to listen to it.

Have fun!

The feedback tasks are designed to be used periodically throughout the course. Ideally learners should record their discussions/talks and listen to short extracts of them with the help of the tasks. Although we have recommended using certain feedback tasks with certain activities, they are a flexible resource. Teachers can therefore refer learners to a particular task if they notice the learner has a problem in the area the task focuses on.

FEEDBACK TASKS

Task	Aims to:	Can be used with:
1	focus on encouraging noises, e.g. *really*	any tasks where learners are sharing personal information, e.g. talking about holidays
2	look at fillers and hesitation devices to improve fluency	any task where a learner is telling an anecdote, e.g. Unit 2 Section 1 Task 4
3	look at how to encourage people to say more	any tasks where learners are exchanging personal information, e.g. Unit 2 Section 2, Unit 3 Section 1 Task 2
4	look at story-telling	Unit 3 Section 3, Unit 4 Section 3 Task 4
5	look at how to make and build on suggestions	any of the Project meetings. Unit 5 Section 2 Task 1, Unit 6 Section 2 Task 4
6	look at how to give opinions	Unit 4 Section 2, Unit 7 Sections 2 and 3
7	look at how we convey disagreement	any task where this arises
8	look at giving a talk	Unit 6 Section 3, Unit 7 Section 4

Task 1

Encouragers

Listen to a short part of your recording in your group.

Can you find examples of expressions like:

Really?
Is that right?
That's nice/interesting/unusual, etc.
It sounds lovely/fascinating/beautiful, etc.

Can you find examples of questions that repeat a key word from what the other person said?

A I usually go windsurfing.
B Windsurfing?

A What's the weather like in Morocco?
B Not too bad but it sometimes rains.
A Rains!
B Yes, I'm afraid so, but it doesn't last long.

These expressions encourage the other person to say more. Try using them next time you have a conversation.

Task 2

Tense/Hesitation devices

Choose about a minute of your recorded story and listen to it again as follows.

First listening   One of you should listen for the verb tenses and the other should listen for vocabulary items. Write down anything which you think was an error or could have been done better. Discuss your notes with your partner and decide how it could have been said better. Ask your teacher to help you if necessary.

Second listening   As you listen see if you can notice any of the things that make continuous speech sound more natural, for example:

hesitation noises such as *erm, mmm, err*
introductory phrases such as *well, so then, anyway, oh*
things which involve the listener in the story such as
so,   you see,   you know,   do you see what I mean?

All of these can help make your speech sound more fluent and natural and native speakers use them all the time. See if you can notice some of them next time you hear some English people talking.

Discuss what you have noted with your partner and decide how and where the telling of the story could be improved by including more of these.

Now do the same for your partner's recording.

Third listening   Finally listen to the recording of the whole of the two stories and tell each other what you liked best about each other's stories.

Task 3

Fluency/encouraging people to say more

Choose a 2–3 minute section of your recording where most people in the class had something to say.

First listening   Listen in particular for questions which people asked to encourage the speaker to say more about him/herself and what he/she did, for example:

So what did you do then?
And did that work?
Do you think you'd do it again?
When did all this happen?
When did you decide to . . . ?

Write down the questions you hear and discuss them with your group.

- Were they grammatically correct?
- Were they suitable? i.e. not too direct or personal.
- Did they help the conversation to develop?

Second listening   Now listen for places in the conversation where there was a break or silence, e.g. where nobody knew what to say next, and discuss these things in your group.

- Was the break natural and acceptable?
- If not, how could you make the conversation continue more fluently? By asking a question? By showing interest? By asking another person's opinion?

Third listening   Listen again to the whole conversation and tell each other which bits you thought were good and which bits showed progress from previous lessons.

Task 4

Story-telling

Compare your recorded story with the story on the cassette. In *Little Red Riding Hood* the story-teller did the following:

- He started with an expression to gain the listeners' attention. What was it? Did you do something similar?
- He changed the speed at which he was talking, i.e. he went slower or faster when he wanted to make the story more exciting or dramatic. Did you?
- The story-teller stressed some words in the story more than others and used his voice to hold the listeners' attention. Can you find an example of this? Did you do it in your story?
- He stopped briefly just before the ending to keep his listeners interested, and to make the ending clear.

Discuss in your group how you could improve your story and try recording it again.

Don't forget to say what was good about the story too!

Task 5

Making/building on suggestions

Choose a 4–5 minute section of your recording when most people had something to say.

First listening   Listen for the ways that people made suggestions. Were any of the following used?

Why don't we . . . ?
We could . . .
I know . . .
How about . . .?

Write down any others that you hear.

Discuss in your group whether the suggestions were grammatically correct and if they could be improved.

Second listening   Listen again and note how people responded to the suggestions. Did they use any of the following expressions?

Yes, that's a good idea.
Yes, and then we could . . .
That's a nice idea, but I don't think . . .

Note down others that you hear.

Decide in your group:

- do the responses build on what the person has said?
- do they stop the conversation?
- do they encourage other people to speak?

If they stop the conversation, decide how they could be improved.

When we work together to produce something it is important that we show we are listening carefully to others and that we try to respond well to what they say, even if we change the idea.

Third listening   Listen to the whole conversation and tell each other when you hear each other using language learnt in previous units.

Task 6

Giving opinions

First listening   Choose a short section of your recorded discussion where everyone in your group had something to say. Listen in particular for the ways in which people introduced their own opinions. For example can you hear any examples of the following?

I think . . .
Well, in my opinion . . .
I believe . . .
As far as I'm concerned . . .
Well, in my country . . .

Write down all the other examples you hear.

Discuss with the group whether the expressions you heard were grammatically correct. Ask your teacher for help if necessary and decide on ways of improving any that were wrong.

Do you think the expressions are used too often in your discussion? Are people listening to each other enough? Or do they sound as though they are only interested in their own opinions?

Discuss possible improvements.

Second listening   Listen again and note down examples of asking for other people's opinions. Can you hear any examples of the following?

What do you think X?
Do you agree?
What's your view?
Is it like that in your country?

Expressions like this involve the other speakers in the discussion and help to make it more fluent and interesting.

Make a list of examples from your recording.

Discuss with the group whether they were grammatically correct and how you might improve any that were wrong.

Decide where more examples of asking for other people's opinions could have been included.

Third listening   Listen again and tell each other about any good bits of conversation you hear, especially examples of language learnt from previous units.

Task 7

Conveying disagreement

First listening Choose a 2–3 minute section in the middle of your discussion where most people in the group had something to say. Listen in particular to the points where one speaker takes over from another. Note down what they say to show that they were listening carefully to the person speaking, before then adding their own opinion, e.g.

That's an interesting idea/point . . .
Yes, I think that's right . . .
Do you really think so?

Listen for points where the change from one person to another sounds sharp or impolite and discuss with your group how it could be improved.

Second listening Listen to your cassette again and note down any examples of language that show the attitude of the speaker to what he/she has heard, e.g. agreement or disagreement.

Particularly where there is disagreement, does the speaker sound abrupt, aggressive or impolite? If so, why?

Would any of the following ways of introducing disagreement help to make the discussion sound more friendly?

Erm, well, I'm not sure about that. Perhaps . . .
I can see why you think that, but . . .
No, I'm sorry, but I don't think that's really true.
Yes, but . . .
I know it's difficult but . . .

Discuss with your group how the discussion might be improved.

Third listening Listen to the whole recording and tell each other when you notice good and interesting bits or examples of some of the language you have been learning.

Task 8

Giving a talk

Exchange your recording of a talk for another group's.

First listening Answer the following questions as you listen.

- Does the talk sound interesting?
- Does it sound fluent?
- Is it easy to understand?

If the answer to any of the questions is 'no' or 'it could be better', try
to decide why. These questions might help you. Discuss them in
your group.

- Are there too many breaks and hesitations?
- Is the voice too flat?
- Is the pronunciation and stress difficult to understand?
- Does the speaker say and do enough to hold the listener's
  attention?
- Is the information presented in an order that is easy to follow?

Try to find examples on the recording to support your decisions and
discuss how you could improve the talk. Ask your teacher for help if
necessary.

Second listening   When we give a talk it is important that it has a
clear beginning, middle and end. This helps us to follow and
understand what the talk is about.

Listen to the talk again and decide which section is the introduction,
which section gives the main information and which is the conclusion.

How did you decide? Write down the words and phrases that helped
to tell you. Did you hear any of the following?

In the introduction

The topic of my talk is . . .
I'd like to begin by . . .
I shall divide my talk into X parts . . .
First of all I'd like to . . .
As an introduction to my talk . . .

In the main body of information

Firstly . . .
Secondly . . .
The advantage of . . .
The disadvantage of . . .
The most important thing to remember is . . .

In the conclusion

I'd like to finish/conclude/summarize by . . .
Let's go through the main points again . . .
I hope that what I have said will . . .

If necessary discuss how the talk could be made clearer.

Third listening   Listen to the talk once more and pick out examples
where you thought the speaker did well. In particular try to find
examples of language learnt in other units.

Get together with the group that has been listening to your talk and
tell each other about your discussion.

TEXT OF THE RECORDINGS

UNIT 1

Section 1   Task 5

How was your holiday?

Lucy   Hello, John! How was your holiday?
John   Oh, er em not too bad.
Lucy   Where was it you went, Morocco?
John   Yes.
Lucy   Oh, was it the first time? Or had you been before?
John   I went briefly as a student some years ago. I must say I didn't like it much but my wife persuaded me to have another go.
Lucy   Oh, and how did you find it this time? It must be a pretty fascinating part of the world.
John   Yes, it is, but it does depend on the kind of holiday you go on.
Lucy   Yes. Er you took the car, did you?
John   No, no actually we hired one when we got there so that we could get around.
Lucy   Oh, I suppose you're a bit like me. I can't stand these all-in package tours that make every country look the same. You know I'm quite interested, I really fancy North Africa, how did you find the place?
John   Oh, well, er, it was a lot better than I remembered from before. Fez was absolutely fascinating but you do need a local guide.
Lucy   Oh, do you, why?
John   Well it's absolutely medieval. It's all narrow streets that haven't changed for hundreds of years.
Lucy   It's one of the main tourist centres, isn't it?
John   Yes, yes and er Marrakesh as well. They're worth a visit.
Lucy   Oh, I bet. Did you find it very expensive? I mean, are they after the tourists' money?
John   Well, yes, in places like Fez and Marrakesh erm its not, cheap. And you have to be prepared to bargain if you want to buy anything. I mean we're glad we went to Fez and Marrakesh but we actually preferred the Atlas Mountains in the South . . .
Lucy   Look, John really you know I, am interested. Do you think we could meet for a drink one evening and have a really long chat . . .

UNIT 2

Section 1   Task 3

An embarrassing moment

When I was a student I went into this shop to buy something. I can't remember now what sort of shop it was. And I bought the thing and there was this shop assistant, this woman standing in front of me and I put my hands in my pockets to get the money and the problem was the trousers I was wearing were rather tight. (laughter) I put both hands in each, both hands in the pockets together to sort of look for the money and as I shoved my hands in these, in the pockets of these tight trousers, suddenly there was a ping (laughter) and there was the top button of these jeans flew through the air and at the same time the zip gently came down. So there I was standing in front of this woman with my hands deep in my pockets with my trousers open at the front. And there was absolutely no way I could hide it because there was no counter in front of us or anything and at the same time I thought well if I take my hands out of my pockets my trousers will fall down but if I dig my hands any deeper into my pockets I'd kinda push them down. (Laughter — So what did you do?) Well, I, I mean by this time I just sweated and blushed a lot and then all I could do was take one hand out of the pocket and kind of pull the zip up with the other and just just all I could think of was I wish I could be outside as fast as possible. I managed to find the money, cos I still had to actually find the money, find the money and it was so obvious because in the end the woman tried to help me a bit because she she vaguely looked over my shoulder rather than looking down to the ground below my waist. (Didn't she laugh?) Well, no, I think she she was as embarrassed as I was and oh goodness I high-tailed it out of that shop as fast as possible. I didn't dare go back for weeks.

UNIT 3

Section 3   Task 2

Little Red Riding Hood

Once upon a time there lived a little girl who was very pretty. Her mother and grandmother loved her very much. Her grandmother made her a very pretty red riding hood which the little girl always wore and she became known as Little Red Riding Hood.

One day her mother baked some cakes. She said 'Go and see your grandmother. She is ill. Take these cakes to her and see how she is. Don't stop on the way.' Grandmother lived in another village and little Red Riding Hood set off with her cakes in a small basket. When she was going through a wood she met a wolf who wanted to eat her. Luckily some woodcutters were nearby so the wolf couldn't. The wolf asked little Red Riding Hood where she was going.

'I'm going to see my grandmother and I'm taking her some cakes my mother made.'

'Does she live far from here?' the wolf asked.

Little Red Riding Hood told the wolf where her grandmother lived and set off towards the house. She did not know that it was dangerous to talk to a wolf and she picked some flowers to put in her basket. The wolf ran to grandmother's house and when he got there he knocked.

'Who's there?'

'It's your granddaughter Little Red Riding Hood. I've brought you some cakes my mother made.'

Grandmother told the wolf how to open the door because she was ill in bed and as soon as the wolf came in he ate her! He was very hungry! The wolf then put on one of grandmother's nightdresses and cap and got in bed to wait for Little Red Riding Hood. Little Red Riding Hood arrived and knocked on the door.

'Who's there?'

When Little Red Riding Hood heard the deep voice she was scared but then she thought her grandmother had a cold. She replied.

'It's your granddaughter, Little Red Riding Hood. I've brought you some flowers and cakes my mother made.'

The wolf softened his voice and said 'Come in. I'm not well and I'm in bed.'

Little Red Riding Hood came in and the wolf hid under the blankets and said 'Put your basket on the table and come and lie down next to me.'

Little Red Riding Hood took off her clothes and got in. She was very surprised to see what her grandmother looked like in her nightdress.

'What big arms you have, grandmother!'

'The better to hug you with, my child.'

'What big legs you have, grandmother!'

'The better to run with, my child.'

'What big ears you have, grandmother!'

'The better to hear you with, my child.'

'What big eyes you have, grandmother!'

'The better to see you with, my child.'

'What big teeth you have, grandmother!'

'The better to eat you.'

With these words the wicked wolf threw himself on Little Red Riding Hood and ate her up.

UNIT 4

Section 1   Task 3

Machu Picchu

Machu Picchu is in the High Andes. It is eight thousand feet up in South America. It was built by the Incas at the height of their empire around 1500 AD. The base of the Inca civilization was agriculture. Potato and maize were cultivated on the terraces on the side of the mountain and potato was so important to the Incas that they invented a way of preserving them by freezing and drying them. Coca which is a plant from which we get cocaine was also grown but only the Inca aristocracy were allowed to chew it. The Incas controlled the irrigation of the dry land below the mountains. They built canals and aquaducts to carry water as well as numerous bridges and roads. They also had messengers and teams of runners carried messages a distance of 240 kilometres a day. Despite this the Incas had no knowledge of the wheel or the arch by AD 1500. They were also unable to read or write. Complicated

messages and records of things like taxes, births, deaths, etc were kept on pieces of string called *quipus*. The system used knots in the string to represent numbers and records were kept of everything and everybody. This was done to control the people and everyone worked for one man — the supreme Inca. He was the head of state as well as a god. The god of the sun.

From 1438 the Incas controlled over four thousand kilometres of coastline from the Andes to the Pacific. But in 1532 a Spaniard, Francisco Pisarro, rode into what is now Peru with 62 horses and 106 foot soldiers and conquered the great empire by capturing the Inca.

UNIT 5

Section 4   Task 1

The Japanese way of bathing

For the Japanese, bathing is one of the pleasures of life. Every Japanese takes one if not two baths a day. At holiday time they'll look for an open-air hot spring pool to relax in and, for the Japanese, the bath can become a social occasion. The traditional Japanese bath also saves on water. No Japanese ever gets into a bath until he has washed himself thoroughly all over. He sits on a small stool in front of the taps and a bowl. He then soaps himself all over and washes his whole body. He then washes all the soap off with the help of bowls of water from the tap. Only then does he get in the bath. In this way the water stays clean and can be used by more than one person. The traditional Japanese bath is large enough for more than one person and often family and friends get into the same bath. For the Japanese the western habit of taking a bath which involves washing in the bath water is vulgar and dirty. This even applies to the open-air hot springs in the country so if you decide to join the Japanese in their favourite holiday pastime make sure you remember to get yourself clean before you get in.

UNIT 6

Section 2   Task 1

An incident abroad

Oh yes, something like that happened to me once er in Spain actually, in Barcelona. I felt very stupid afterwards. I'd just arrived in Barcelona on business and after checking into my hotel I decided to go for a walk down the main street erm just to get the feel of the place again and as I was window shopping minding my own business a man came up to me and looked very worried sounded very worried and said 'Oh, excuse me. Do you speak English?' And I said 'Yes, I do.' but also realized that er from his accent that he was German and so I, having lived in Germany, I spoke to him in German and he explained to me that er he and his friend had been staying in a hotel in Barcelona and the night before they had had everything stolen from their hotel room, all their money, all their belongings, everything. And they had been at the German Consulate all day er trying to get through to Germany in the hope of having some money sent and by this time it

was about 6.30 in the evening and he said the Consulate
had been totally unsuccessful and he and his friend had no
money. They hadn't eaten all day. They didn't know what
they were going to do. They were terribly worried and
could I possibly help them by giving them some money
and I thought for a moment and I thought well he seems
very genuine. He's well dressed, well spoken, quite
friendly. Erm seemed intelligent and I thought well I'm
sure if I gave him some money he'd give it back to me and
so I said well Yes, Ok and I opened my purse and I gave
him a hundred peseta note. Er not being used to the
money because I'd only just arrived I thought well a
hundred peseta note is really quite a lot of money and I
said well if you'd like to give it back I'm living at that hotel
down the road. He wrote the name of the hotel down and
said oh yes, you know, he'd bring it back and so on. And
er we parted and er a few minutes later I was sitting in a
cafe having a cup of coffee thinking about the whole
incident and I began to realise how very stupid I'd been.
Not only was 100 pesetas in fact very little money. It was
only about 70 or 80p. That made me feel guilty that I'd
asked for it back believe it or not but I also realized that
the whole thing had just been a confidence trick and I
would never see the money again.

KEY

UNIT 1

1   What sort of person are you?

Task 2
Score 1–4 points for each of your answers and add up the total.

	a	b	c	d	e
1	1	3	4	4	2
2	4	1	2	3	
3	4	3	1	2	
4	4	1	2	1	
5	2	4	1	3	
6	4	1	3	2	

Score
20–24   You are adventurous. People and excitement are important to you all the time.
15–19   You are hardworking and serious normally but you enjoy a change when on holiday.
10–14   Holidays are all right as long as you get what you want. You are a conservative.
6–10   You are quiet and enjoy being alone.

UNIT 2

1   Sharing experiences

Task 3
1 The man bought something.
   He put both hands in his pockets.
   He lost the top button from his trousers.
   He took the money out of his pocket.
   He left the shop quickly.
2 F, T, F, F, T

UNIT 3

2   Time is money

Task 1
1 b,   2 c,   3 a,   4 d

3   Stories for our time

Task 3
The stories are *The boy who cried 'wolf'*, *The goose that laid the golden eggs*, *The fox and the crow*.

UNIT 5

4   The pleasures of life — Japanese style

Task 5
Kabuki
Kabuki is a form of traditional Japanese theatre which was started by a woman in the early seventeenth century. In 1667, however, trouble with the actors meant women were not allowed on the stage and even today all the parts are played by men. An individual performance usually lasts more than six hours but people usually go and see a series of plays during a week. Spectators can come and go during the performance and the stories are well known. An orchestra of traditional instruments and a chorus accompanies the action and provides the atmosphere.

The tea ceremony
'Chanoyu' or the tea ceremony is Buddist in origin. It became a ritual in the fourteenth century and it is a search for beauty and control which is still followed today. The ceremony takes several hours and there are strict rules: the 'suki' or tea house must be in a landscaped garden; the teahouse needs to be decorated in certain ways; there is an order for making and serving, e.g. the tea is served to the most important guest first, etc.

Sumo
'Sumo' is Japanese wrestling which started over 2000 years ago. The wrestlers are huge men of 130 kg or more. They train in special schools and eat large amounts of fish and rice to put on weight. The important matches are shown on television and sumo wrestling is a national sport. The wrestlers fight in a 5-metre ring. They try to throw the opponent on his back or out of the ring. The referee is dressed as a shinto priest because sumo wrestlers used to fight in temples and sumo wrestling has many traditions.

UNIT 7

1   Dreams to remember

Task 3
Psychologists suggest that there are three important symbols in the picture. Blake was a writer so the sea is the unconscious where ideas come from. The walk up the mountain represents the struggle through life. The woman represents inspiration and encouragement to carry on.

2   The American dream

Task 1
The American dream refers to equality of opportunity.
The theory is that in America anyone can become
President and this is referred to as the American dream.
Whether this is true or not is a subject of much discussion.

3   A dream society?

Task 3
The photograph shows a family of dustbowl refugees
during the 1930s' Depression in America. Langston
Hughes (1902–1967) was a negro writer who wrote about
social problems and the poem was published in 1932.

UNIT 8

2   The natural way

Task 1
a 6, b 5, c 2, d 4, e 1, f 3.